SOULFUL MURMURS

VERSES FROM UNSPOILED HEART

PARTH PRITI KHAJGIWALE

Made with ♥ on the Notion Press Platform
www.notionpress.com

__To All Those Who Have Shaped My Journey,__

To Almighty Lord,

In the light's embrace, your teachings find space.

Gratitude flows for the creativity you've bestowed,

My Mumma and Baba, my guiding stars,

Your love and wisdom, who you are.

To Prof. Minal Badgujar, mentor and guide,

Soft skills honed, you're always by my side.

This book is tribute to each one's part,

Shaping my character, with love in my heart.

Contents

Contents

Preface

In the hushed passageways of the heart, where laughter's echoes and the shadows of innocence endure, *"Soulful Murmurs: Verses from Unspoiled Heart"* reveals itself. This anthology is a collage of poetic expressions that explore the raw and unfiltered depths of our innermost sanctuaries.

Within these pages, you'll encounter the delicate choreography of emotions presented in various poetic forms—free verse, prose, sonnet, and acrostic—all harmonising to narrate the journey of a soul striving to preserve its inherent purity. The title, *"Soulful Murmurs,"* itself encourages readers to listen closely to the heart's whispers, to the subtle rhythm of a spirit untarnished by the clamour of the world.

At its essence, this compilation seeks to unravel the layers concealing the core of our existence. Beyond the tears, beyond the anger, lies a tender truth—a child within, earnestly working to spread joy and evoke pride in the hearts of others. These verses encapsulate the fragility of our inner worlds, resonating with the universal chord of humanity.

The choice of poetic forms reflects the multifaceted nature of our emotions, echoing the diverse landscapes of our experiences. Free verse meanders through the uncharted territories of the soul, prose weaves narratives, sonnets echo with structured beauty, and acrostics spell out silent truths. These poems are unarranged and unorganized, as presenting them in any order would be an insult to human life; every page, every verse is a new day with different emotions.

Additionally, I am delighted to introduce *"Emerging Voices,"* a distinguished section within *"Soulful Murmurs."* Meticulously curated, this section highlights the creative endeavors of burgeoning writers. It serves as a platform for aspiring authors to showcase their work and expand their audience. Our primary aim is to nurture and bolster emerging talents within the writing community, offering them an invaluable opportunity for exposure and recognition.

"Soulful Murmurs" extends an invitation to embark on a contemplative journey—a pilgrimage into the sacred recesses of the self. It is a celebration of vulnerability, an ode to the undying spirit that endures, unspoiled, beneath the weight of life's complexities.

May these verses function as a mirror, reflecting the reader's own reflections and resonances. May they evoke recognition and stir the dormant echoes of the unspoiled heart within each of us.

As you peruse the pages, may you find solace, inspiration, and perhaps a mirror reflecting your own soulful murmurs.

Parth Priti Khajgiwale

Acknowledgements

In the inception of this literary endeavor, I find myself humbled, acknowledging the paramount presence of the Supreme Personality of Godhead, Lord Krishna. His divine guidance has been a masterpiece of inspiration, infusing my life with wisdom, purpose, and strength beyond measure. To the Eternal One, I offer my deepest gratitude for His unwavering grace and influence.

To my family, the cornerstone of my existence, I extend a profound acknowledgment. My fighter mother and father, your boundless love and unwavering support have been instrumental in shaping the narrative of my life. In your embrace, I have found strength, solace, and a profound sense of purpose. I also wish to honor my supportive brother, whose steadfast presence and encouragement have always stood by my decisions.

Special thanks to Vanika Sangtani, whose positive affirmation *"Hum Kar Lenge Yaar!"* has been a beacon of motivation. Your belief in my capabilities has been a constant source of encouragement.

In the realm of personal and professional development, I stand indebted to the exceptional mentorship of Prof. Minal Badgujar, whose guidance has been a masterpiece of encouragement and transformation. Your dedication to nurturing my soft skills and your unwavering belief in my potential have sculpted my journey in profound ways.

The mosaic of my life's journey also includes the influence of numerous individuals, both direct and indirect, who have enriched my experiences. I am particularly grateful to the *Emerging Voices* authors: *Vishakha Deshpande, Sujal Musale, Sahiti Ramadugu, Shravani Bante, Arya Katre, Shara Tadas, and Vedant Jagtap.* Each of you has woven threads of inspiration and learning into the fabric of my existence, making this literary creation possible.

Lastly, to the readers and supporters of my work, I extend my sincere gratitude. Your engagement and enthusiasm are the canvas upon which my words find resonance and purpose. It is your encouragement that fuels my creative endeavors and drives me to continue sharing my thoughts and experiences with the world.

To all those who have played a part in my life, I express my heartfelt thanks for the indelible marks you have left on my journey. You are the brushstrokes that paint the masterpiece of my life, and for that, I am eternally grateful.

With deepest gratitude,
   Parth Priti Khajgiwale

1. Maa we're not late

•

Maa we're not late,
I whispered my words
a gentle assurance
against the rush of time.

Her eyes, etched with
lines of worry,
softened slightly
as she looked at me.

The world outside may
at relentless pace,
but in that moment,
it felt as if we had
captured a piece of eternity.

The hands of the clock
could no longer bind us;
what matters was the shared journey,
the quiet understanding between us.

Time with all its insistence,
could wait. We had each other

And that was enough.

"In the rush of time, a whispered assurance captured eternity, for we had each other, and that was enough."

2. I cried that day...

I wept that day, not with the fury of a storm,
nor thunderous wails shaking the earth's core.
My tears flowed like gentle rain,
kissing fragile flower petals.

A quiet weeping, an intimate unveiling
of emotions long hidden within.

In solitude, I faced echoes of lost innocence,
a vulnerability cloaked in adulthood's armor.
These tears weren't weakness,
but resilience of the inner child,
whose laughter once filled my heart.

For dreams wilted and fantasies faded,
replaced by grown-up practicalities.
The world taught walls, shielding
from unpredictable storms.
Yet, in tears, walls crumbled,
revealing raw spirit untouched by time.

Not just sorrow, but joy and longing merged,
a bittersweet symphony of nostalgia.

I wept for the lost magic,
the unfiltered wonder of yesteryears.

Each tear revealed untarnished beauty,
the enduring purity of my core.
In vulnerability, I found treasures
untouched by time's harsh winds.

As the last tear fell,
it carried the world's weight,
briefly dimming my inner light.
But in that release, I found strength,
a celebration of enduring innocence.

I wept, not in defeat,
but as homage to my inner flame,
still flickering softly within.

**"May these verses embrace you in the warmth of
shared tears, inviting you to rediscover the echoes of
your own inner innocence."**

3. I made a mistake...

In the quiet of night, amid whispered secrets,
Where darkness and light dance in silent waltz,
In the depths of my own innocence's glow,
I find solace as dawn's light breaks.

In the maze of life's uncertain paths,
I've stumbled, straying from the intended way,
Yet deep within, where sincerity resides,
A stream flows, its current steady and pure.

For within our imperfections lies wisdom,
A story woven into the fabric of existence,
Each misstep a chapter in the journey,
Granting us strength to pursue our greater purpose.

Let errors guide us, not bind us,
To the core of our humanity, where hope endures.

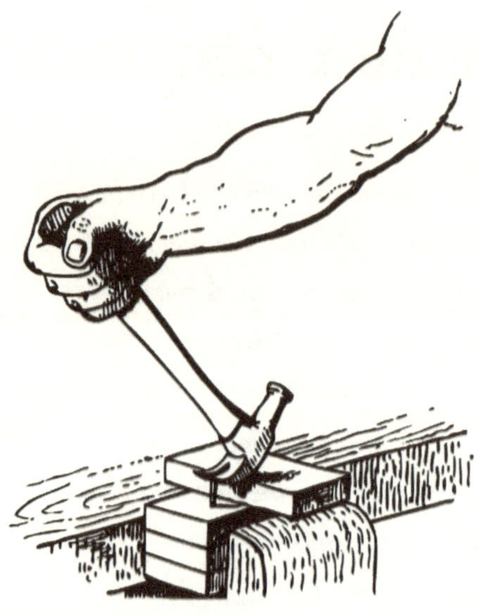

"In every mistake, find the compassionate thread of inner innocence, weaving a tapestry of growth and understanding."

4. Something that I crave for…

In the unsounded stretches between solitude,
a thirst lingers, not for attention's blaze,
but for the subtle nectar of kindness.

A hunger for love simmers beneath the surface,
seeking sustenance in the simplicity of connection.
Craving care, my soul navigates the landscape of yearning,
a seeker in the vast expanse of human warmth.

In the symphony of unspoken desires,
an anthem emerges—a declaration of concern
for those orbiting the circumference of my existence.
These unspoken notes resonate with the innocent chords that bind
us,
a melody of empathy in the chaotic cacophony of emotions.

The dance of emotions unfolds, a ballet
of delicate balance, where self-sufficiency
entwines with the need for shared warmth.
The desire for love emerges not as a grand spectacle,
but as an understated yearning,
a thread weaving through the fabric of my being,

connecting me to the collective vulnerability of all souls.

As these words sketch the canvas of inner innocence,
may they evoke a resonance within the reader's core.
Let tears flow like a cleansing rain,
for in vulnerability, we find the shared pulse of our humanity—
a yearning for love, kindness, and the authentic care
that unites us all.

"*In moments alone, I long for simple kindness, a warmth that connects us in the silent dance of shared humanity.*"

5. Through the Eyes of Child

In a child's sparkling gaze,
I found pure innocence,
where errors were fleeting shadows,
and the world bloomed with wonder.

In the playground of youth, I danced freely,
my missteps mere ripples
in a sea of endless possibilities.
Laughter drowned out whispers of mistakes.

But adolescence arrived tumultuous,
and peers' eyes revealed my misjudgments.
In their reflection, I saw my folly,
and innocence bore smudges of experience.

Insecurities spoke through the mirror,
missteps became stumbling blocks
in the quest for belonging,
where fitting in became an art to master.

Now, as an adult, I reflect,
the child's gaze replaced by wisdom.

In life's mosaic, I see patterns
and trace growth through folly.

Mistakes, seen through time's lens,
are not missteps but journeys of discovery.
To a child, they're passing clouds;
to a teen, fragments of identity.

Yet, as adults, we grasp inner innocence,
the resilient core amidst judgment's storms.
Mistakes aren't stains but brushstrokes
on the soul's canvas.

For in the eyes of the child, the teen, the adult,
mistakes aren't endings but chapters turned,
stories woven in time's fabric,
where inner innocence endures.

"Embrace mistakes, cherish growth."

6. I know I am not Alone, But...

I know I am not alone, but a wanderer unguided,
In the realm of pure untouched, where echoes softly glide.
Through fields unnamed, with sunlight on my face,
A dance of dreams unfolding, in this uncharted space.

No threads of cynic weave through the fabric of my mind,
As I traverse unmarked trails, uncertainty to find.
In innocence, a child, unburdened by the weight,
Of shadows looming large, yet to seal my fate.

No fortress of experience, no walls of guarded doubt,
Just meadows stretching endless, where whispers linger, stout.
In the company of breezes, with nature as my kin,
I journey through the untouched, where the journey does begin.

Not shackled by echoes of the past or future's call,
I float on the river of now, a silent waterfall.
No relentless tempests disturb the calm within,
A sacred sanctuary where naivety is akin.

The world may hide its corners, in corners yet unseen,
Yet here in this cocoon, the canvas is pristine.

I know I am not alone, in this uncharted domain,
A symphony of innocence, an everlasting refrain.

"*In the realm of the unguided wanderer, where whispers linger stout, I float on the river of now, a silent waterfall—no shadows looming, no relentless tempests disturb the calm within. The canvas is pristine, a symphony of innocence, an everlasting refrain.*"

7. The Day I'll depart...

Upon the horizon of life's twilight, I reflect
on innocence bound to the day I'll depart—
when the pulse of a once-vibrant heart
yields to the quiet cadence of finality.

In the corridors of my soul, laughter echoes,
a resilient anthem of moments untouched
by the tarnish of worldly complexities.
The garden within, where joy once blossomed,
now stands as a testament to the transient nature
of untamed dreams.

Shadows linger, casting contemplative hues
upon the narrative of my existence.
The day I'll die unfolds, not with ceremonial solemnity,
but with graceful surrender to the inevitable.
It's not feared, but met with bittersweet acknowledgment—
a waltz between ephemeral and eternal.

Threads of resilience weave through the fabric
of vulnerability, creating a mosaic of memories,
a raw portrayal of unfiltered life.
The day I'll die is a palette of muted and vivid strokes,

a composition encapsulating the essence
of a soul unburdened.

As the sun sets on this chapter, may the hues
of remembered laughter and echoes of love
be brushstrokes painting the final scene.
In traversing the delicate threshold between life
and the unknown, may inner innocence linger—
A quiet resonance in the expanse of past and yet-to-be.

"In life's departure, find celebration, not lamentation. Dance with the enduring spirit of an untamed soul."

8. Someday I'll just run away and leave everyone...

In the depths of my thoughts, stirs a longing,
A distant echo of escape from woven complexities.
Someday, the yearning to break free,
May lead me on a journey, shedding ties to reality.

Seeking untouched sanctuary, where my soul dances freely,
Unburdened by worldly demands, untouched purity.
I envision a departure fueled by desire,
To rediscover the wild landscapes of self, untouched by fire.

In the silence of introspection, flickers a quiet flame,
Inner innocence beneath layers of experience.
Stepping into the wilderness of self-discovery,
Curiosity drives my stride, marking paths with footprints.

Not born of resentment, but of raw authenticity,
Unveiling the essence obscured by time and trials.
Escape isn't rejection, but pilgrimage,
Guided by intuition's sage, to the heart's core.

In the cocoon of self-exploration, I weave,
Fragments of inner innocence into my evolving tale.

Embracing untarnished reflections of self,
Solace found beneath the open sky's vast expanse.

Someday, beneath the open sky's mirrored expanse,
Not to leave all behind, but to return to myself.
A pilgrimage to reclaim innocence's essence,
Where pure reflections ripple through life's corridors.

"In the silent journey within, I yearn to break free, rediscovering the wild landscapes of self where unblemished purity dances, untouched by the world's demands."

9. Hey, let's chat for a while...

Hey there, let's have a chat,
Underneath the willow tree where we sat.
Stories untold, songs yet unsung,
In the garden where dreams are sprung.

Among the whispers of the old oak trees,
Where secrets sway in the evening breeze.
A painting of colors, soft and bright,
In the fading light of day and night.

No need for masks, no need to hide,
Just honest talks, side by side.
Through fields of words we've never said,
Let's walk where the songbird's led.

A melody woven with threads of time,
In moments simple, yet so sublime.
The sun shares stories of its day,
As the moon dances in its gentle way.

Not in whispers or quiet embrace,
But in laughter that fills this space.

Moments pure, untouched and kind,
In the tapestry of our shared mind.

So, let's turn a page, share a tale,
In this fleeting moment, let's set sail.
No need for secrets or hidden themes,
Just two hearts talking under moonlight beams.

For in this exchange of words and grace,
Lies the magic that time can't erase.
In the quiet corners where truth resides,
Let's chat for a while, let our souls collide.

"Let's talk under the trees, where stories and laughter create magic."

10. I'm scared...

In the silent folds of night's embrace,
A fear unfurls, a specter takes its place.
Alone, I tremble in the shroud of the unknown,
Dreading the loss of love that I've known.

Heartbeats echo in the chamber of my fears,
A symphony of doubts, a cascade of tears.
Will love's melody dissolve in the void,
Leaving me stranded, shattered, and devoid?

Loved ones, like whispers in the wind,
Their presence a treasure, a world within.
Yet time, relentless, steals the tender light,
Leaving only the residue of a fading night.

Creativity, a wild fire within my chest,
What if it dwindles, a mere shadow at best?
Passion, a river coursing through my veins,
Anxiety lingers, threatening to break the chains.

People, celestial bodies in my life's expanse,
Their departure, a cosmic and cruel dance.
Stars that once sparkled in my soul's night,

Fading away, leaving me in solitude's bite.

In the labyrinth of fears, shadows dance,
I yearn for a sanctuary, a fleeting chance.
Yet darkness murmurs its dissonant song,
A haunting melody where I don't belong.

In the core of this fear, a spark persists,
A glint of defiance, where courage exists.
For even in love's inevitable decay,
Strength emerges in the absence of dismay.

"In night's silent embrace, fear unfurls and love's melody echoes in the void, yet in the labyrinth of fears, a spark of defiance persists, revealing strength where courage exists."

11. Will I be alright?

Will I be alright?
In the quiet of my restless mind,
I ponder the unknown,
Grasping at threads of uncertainty.

Questions swirl like autumn leaves,
Fluttering in the tempest of doubt,
Yet beneath the tumult,
A whisper of resilience persists.

Will I be alright?
In the labyrinth of my fears,
I search for fragments of hope,
Tracing the contours of my vulnerability.

The echoes of past struggles linger,
A reminder of battles fought,
But amidst the scars,
I find strength in resilience.

Will I be alright?
In the shadows of doubt,
I confront the specter of uncertainty,

Navigating the maze of my existence.

Each step a testament to resilience,
Each breath a defiance against despair,
For in the depths of uncertainty,
I find the courage to believe:

Yes, I will be alright.

"In the labyrinth of my fears, I confront the specter of uncertainty, navigating the maze of my existence. Each step a testament to resilience, each breath a defiance against despair. For in the depths of uncertainty, I find the epitome of courage: Yes, I will be alright."

12. I am Rich

I am Rich.
Not in the glint of gold,
Nor in the sheen of silver,
But in the quiet depth of my soul.
Richness, not in riches stacked,
But in the warmth of simple joys,
In the abundance of gratitude.

I am Rich.
Not in towering buildings,
Nor in lavish cars that gleam,
But in the whispers of contentment.
Richness, not in material gains,
But in the simplicity of needs met,
In the serenity of acceptance.

I am Rich.
Not in the clamor of possessions,
Nor in the pursuit of endless wants,
But in the freedom from desire.
Richness, not in the quest for more,
But in the richness of the present,
In the treasure of inner peace.

I am Rich.
Rich in the laughter of loved ones,
Rich in the embrace of nature's wonders,
Rich in the moments of pure bliss.
For richness resides not in opulence,
But in the soul's liberation from longing,
In the embrace of life's true essence.

A Tribute To Our Legendary Founder

Late Shri Pralhad P. Chhabria

13. What if she says no?

In the quiet of doubt, the question arises,
"What if she says no?" amidst silent sighs.
But within the courage to confront the unknown,
Lies the strength to reap what's sown.

For what if she says yes, in that tender reply,
A universe of possibilities, reaching the sky.
No matter the outcome, you dared to try,
In the echo of honesty, you begin to fly.

Acknowledge her truth, if it's a gentle decline,
Move forward with grace, your heart's design.
And if it's a yes, let jubilance shine,
Embrace the moment, in love's sweet sign.

Regret finds no foothold, in the courage you display,
For in asking, you pave a bold new way.
So, with fervor and hope, let your voice convey,
"What if?" - the beginning of a brighter day.

14. Nostalgia For Youth

In the quiet moments between dusk and dawn,
when shadows dance on the walls
like echoes of forgotten laughter,
nostalgia tiptoes into the chambers of the heart,
whispering tales of youthful exuberance.
It is a tender ache,
a bittersweet symphony
that plays softly in the depths of memory.

In the sepia-toned corridors of the mind,
we wander through the gardens of yesteryears,
where innocence bloomed like wildflowers
beneath the azure sky.
We recall the reckless abandon of our youth,
when every day was an adventure waiting to unfold,
and the world was a canvas
upon which we painted our dreams.

Oh, how we yearn for the days
when time was but a gentle breeze,
and responsibilities were distant shores
on an endless horizon.
We long for the embrace of friends

whose faces have faded with the passing of seasons,
and for the warmth of embraces
shared beneath the stars.

In the hush of midnight reverie,
we summon fragments of our past
like fireflies in the darkness,
clinging to fleeting moments
as if they were treasures to be cherished.
We smile at the innocence of our folly,
the bravery of our dreams,
and the sweetness of our loves lost and found.

But nostalgia is a gentle thief,
stealing away the sharp edges of reality
and leaving behind a softened, rose-tinted lens
through which we view our past.
We remember the laughter, but forget the tears.
We recall the triumphs, but overlook the trials.
And in our longing for what once was,
we sometimes forget to embrace what is.

Yet, amidst the wistful sighs and whispered regrets,
there is a beauty in the nostalgia for youth.
It is a testament to the richness of life,
to the depth of human experience,
and to the enduring power of memory.

For even as the years slip through our fingers
like grains of sand,
the echoes of our youth linger on,
etched forever in the recesses of our souls.

"In the quiet moments between dusk and dawn, nostalgia tiptoes into the heart, whispering tales of youthful exuberance. It is a bittersweet symphony, a testament to the richness of life and the enduring power of memory."

15. Fragile Strength

In the naked expanse of vulnerability,
I stand, stripped of armor, bare to the core,
Exposed to the elements of judgment and fear.

Every nerve a wire,
Every emotion a storm,
I navigate this fragile landscape,
Where the slightest breeze can shatter me.

It's in the rawness of my being,
In the tender flesh of my truth,
That I find my vulnerability,
A mirror reflecting my humanity.

For it is not weakness,
But the strength to feel deeply,
To bleed openly,
To love fiercely,
That renders me vulnerable.

In this world of sharp edges and harsh realities,
I am a softness,
A vulnerability woven into the fabric of my existence.

And though it may leave me open,
To pain, to hurt, to rejection,
It also opens me,
To connection, to empathy, to growth.

So I embrace this vulnerability,
Not as a burden,
But as a gift,
A reminder of my humanity,
In a world that often forgets.

"Vulnerability is not weakness, but the strength to feel deeply and love fiercely. I embrace it as a gift, a reminder of my humanity in a world that often forgets."

16. Ephemeral Bonds

In the quiet gaze, I find solace, a sanctuary
where words are whispered in the silence between us.
Your presence, a symphony of untold stories,
traces of laughter etched in the corners of your eyes.

I see your eyebrows, meticulously crafted arches,
each curve a testament to beauty undefined,
and your lips, a masterpiece of gentle curves,
the echo of a smile that paints the world anew.

Your hair, a cascade of memories,
falling softly as you recline,
a tender embrace of midnight hues,
a canvas for whispered dreams.

I am not your lover, but I am your confidant,
a silent witness to your joys and sorrows,
a soul bound to yours in quiet understanding,
a bond deeper than words can weave.

In the depths of our conversations,
I find refuge from the storms of life,
each word a lifeline in the tumultuous sea,

each moment a testament to our shared humanity.

And though the odds may not be in my favor,
and the stars may not align for us,
I cherish the moments we share,
knowing that in your heart, I find home.

So let me be your friend, your companion,
walking beside you through the passage of time,
holding your hand through laughter and tears,
a steadfast presence till the end of days.

And when the final curtain falls,
and shadows dance upon the stage,
may you remember the moments we shared,
and shed a tear for the friend who loved you well.

"In the serene glance, I find peace, a sanctuary where unspoken stories unfold."

17. Isolation or Validation

In the void, a solitary figure stands,
Eclipsed by the shadows of doubt,
Lost in the endless expanse of uncertainty.

Yearning for a nod of recognition,
A flicker of understanding,
Yet finding only the echo of their own voice,
Lost in the vastness of indifference.

Validation becomes the elusive mirage,
Dancing just beyond their reach,
A tantalizing dream that slips through grasping fingers,
Leaving behind the ache of unfulfilled longing.

Isolation, a silent companion,
A weight that presses upon weary shoulders,
As they navigate the desolate landscape of their mind,
Seeking refuge in the echoes of their own thoughts.

"Validation fades; isolation endures deeply."

18. Threshold of Existence

Close to the edge of existence,
hovering on the brink,
where shadows dance with light's last flicker,
and time's grasp loosens its hold.

Breath, a fragile thread,
weaving between realms,
where the pulse of life whispers faintly,
and the threshold of mortality beckons.

In the twilight between dusk and dawn,
where dreams dissolve into the ether,
and the symphony of life's symphony fades,
a fragile soul lingers, clinging to the edge.

In the hollow echo of mortality's call,
where echoes of the past fade to whispers,
and the future stretches into the unknown,
there lies a paradox of being.

Living the death, yet not dead,
an ephemeral dance with fate,
where every heartbeat is a defiance,

and every moment a testament to resilience.

In the symphony of existence's final note,
where the crescendo of life meets its end,
therein lies the beauty of the paradox,
of being close to death, yet living the death.

"Hovering on the brink of existence, where shadows dance with light's last flicker, a fragile soul lingers, living the death yet not dead—a testament to resilience and the beauty of the paradox."

19. A Verse on Grace

In whispers soft, the world confides
Its secrets, hidden deep inside.
Amidst the chaos, there's a grace,
A tranquil calm, a sacred space.

Behold the art of simplicity,
A melody in sweet serenity.
In every line, in every rhyme,
A timeless truth, a paradigm.

In nature's canvas, pure and bright,
The sun sets low, the stars ignite.
No need for grandeur, pomp, or show,
In humble beauty, hearts aglow.

The gentle breeze, a soothing sigh,
Underneath the vast, open sky.
No need for words to complicate,
In silence, we appreciate.

A single flower, blooming bright,
In modest hues, it brings delight.
No need for excess, no need for more,

In its simplicity, we adore.

In laughter shared, in moments small,
In simple acts, we find it all.
No need for riches to define,
In love's embrace, our souls entwine.

So let us learn this sacred art,
To simplify and ease the heart.
In quiet moments, we shall see,
The beauty found in simplicity.

"In whispers soft, the world confides its secrets, revealing the grace in simplicity. Amidst chaos, a timeless truth shines: in humble beauty and quiet moments, we find the essence of life."

20. Why should I let her go?

In the quiet corridors of your heart,
echoes the question, a whisper,
"Why should I let her go?"

She dances in your thoughts,
a haunting melody of memories,
entwined with laughter and tears.

But there's a weight, isn't there?
A burden you carry, unseen yet heavy,
clinging to your every step.

She's a wildfire, fierce and untamed,
a tempest in your tranquil sea,
threatening to consume all in her path.

Yet, in her warmth, you found solace,
in her chaos, a semblance of order,
and in her eyes, a reflection of your own desires.

But love, it's not always enough,
sometimes it's letting go that's the hardest part,

to set free what was never truly yours.

For in the letting go,
lies the chance for growth,
the opportunity to find yourself anew.

So, release her gently,
like a bird from its cage,
and watch as she soars into the unknown.

For in her freedom,
you may just find your own,
and in the letting go,
discover the peace you've longed for.

"In the release, find your own wings to soar."

21. Disturbed Minds Seek Peace and Solace

In the depths of chaos, a quiet plea,
Disturbed minds seek peace and solace,
Amidst the clamor of their own creation.

In the flurry of thoughts, a tangled web,
Caught in the maze of uncertainty,
Yearning for a moment of stillness.

The unspoiled heart, a beacon of hope,
Amidst the storm, a sanctuary,
Offering refuge to the weary soul.

In the gentle embrace of nature's arms,
Where the rustle of leaves whispers secrets,
And the melody of birds sings of freedom.

In the hush of dawn's first light,
Where the world awakens with a sigh,
And possibilities stretch out like endless horizons.

Here, in the quiet spaces,
Disturbed minds find solace,

In the embrace of simplicity,
In the unspoiled heart's gentle rhythm.

"In the depths of chaos, disturbed minds seek peace amidst their own creation. In the quiet spaces and nature's embrace, they find solace, discovering hope in the unspoiled heart's gentle rhythm."

22. Let's have a call

In the chambers of our lives,
voices ricochet off walls,
lost in the tumult of existence.

Let's connect, even briefly,
within the expanse of a two-hour call.
Listen to me,
not just my words,
but the silent yearnings of my soul.

In the whirlwind of days,
time slips through our grasp,
moments fleeting, scarcely noticed.
Yet in those precious minutes,
I crave your attention,
a haven for my thoughts,
a sanctuary for my heart.

I seek someone to hear,
to catch the whispers of my dreams,
the echoes of my fears,
the melodies of my desires.

So let's converse,
not tethered by the clock,
but by the desire to bond,
to share, to comprehend,
to be acknowledged in the vast landscape
of this clamorous world.

In the chambers of our lives,
voices bounce off walls,
lost in the cacophony of existence.

Let's have a call,
even if just for five minutes,
in the expanse of a two-hour stretch.
Listen to me,
not just the words I utter,
but the silent symphonies of my soul.

In the rush of everyday,
time slips through our fingers like sand,
moments fleeting, barely noticed.
But in those precious minutes,
I crave your attention,
a sanctuary for my thoughts,
a refuge for my heart.

I want someone to listen,
to hear the whispers of my dreams,
the echoes of my fears,
the melodies of my desires.

So let's have a call,
not bound by the clock,
but by the yearning to connect,
to share, to understand,
to be heard in the vast expanse
of this noisy world.

"In the cacophony of life, let's make time for connection. Even in a brief moment, listening becomes a sanctuary for the soul, where whispers find ears and hearts find solace."

23. Final Slumber

In the quiet realm where dreams embrace,
A whispered wish, a silent grace,
I ponder on life's endless sweep,
And wonder if someday, I'll just go to sleep.

In the hush of night, where shadows play,
I contemplate the end of day,
A gentle slumber, deep and sweet,
Perhaps, one day, it'll be my final retreat.

With weary eyes and a soul so worn,
I dream of a place where I'll be reborn,
Where earthly worries cease to keep,
And in that sleep, perhaps, I'll forever sleep.

No more to wake to morning's light,
No more to wrestle with the night,
Just a peaceful rest, eternal and deep,
As I surrender to the stillness, in endless sleep.

But in this moment, as I muse and ponder,
I find solace in the stars up yonder,
For life's a journey, winding and steep,

And though someday I may sleep, I'll cherish the moments I keep.

For every laugh, for every tear,
For every joy, for every fear,
Each heartbeat, each breath, a treasure to reap,
Until the day I drift into eternal sleep.

So let me live with purpose and with grace,
Embracing each moment, in this wondrous place,
For though someday I'll just go to sleep,
I'll leave behind a legacy, for others to keep.

"Someday I'll just go to sleep, and perhaps, never awaken."

24. Eye for an I

In the heart of a bustling city,
amidst the cacophony of voices
and the ceaseless motion of bodies,
there exists a solitary figure.
She walks with purpose,
yet beneath the confident stride
lies a quiet uncertainty,
a subtle tremor of doubt
that echoes in the recesses of her mind.

Surrounded by a multitude of eyes,
each one a silent judge,
she navigates the streets with a careful awareness,
acutely conscious of the scrutiny
that follows her every move.
These eyes, they doubt her,
question her,
dissecting her every word, her every action,
searching for flaws to confirm their suspicions.

But amidst the sea of doubting gazes,
there is one eye she seeks above all others -
the eye within herself.

It is the eye that sees beyond the superficial,
beyond the façade she presents to the world.
It is the eye that knows her deepest fears and boldest dreams,
the eye that bears witness to the truth of her being.

And so she turns inward,
delving into the depths of her own soul
in search of that elusive eye.
She confronts the shadows that lurk within,
the doubts and insecurities that threaten to engulf her.
She stares into the abyss of her own self-doubt,
refusing to look away,
refusing to surrender to the voices of dissent
that clamor for her attention.

In this journey of self-discovery,
she uncovers the beauty that lies hidden beneath the surface,
the strength that lies dormant within her.
She embraces her flaws as facets of her humanity,
her scars as testament to her resilience.
She learns to love herself
not in spite of her imperfections, but because of them.

And as she emerges from the depths of her own soul,
she finds herself transformed.
No longer bound by the expectations of others,
no longer shackled by the chains of doubt,

she stands tall and unyielding,
a beacon of self-assurance in a world of uncertainty.

For she has found the eye that sees the 'I' within her,
the eye that knows her true worth.
And in that knowledge,
she finds the strength to defy the doubting eyes that surround her,
to embrace the fullness of who she is,
unapologetically and unequivocally.

Image Credits : IG @create_witharya

25. I am the Door

In the quiet chambers of the soul,
Where whispers dance with shadows bold,
I am the sentinel, the silent guide,
Carving pathways where secrets hide.

With hinges forged from time's embrace,
I stand as witness, a sacred space,
Where verses flow from unspoiled heart,
Each word a beacon, a gentle art.

Through me, the weary find their rest,
Seekers of truth, by doubts oppressed.
I am the threshold, the boundary line,
Between what's lost and what's divine.

Inscribed upon my wooden frame,
Echoes of those who sought the same,
To enter, to transcend, to be reborn,
In the verses from an unspoiled morn.

I am the Door, both open and closed,
Guardian of stories yet to be composed.
Step through, brave soul, into the unknown,

For in these verses, your heart finds home.

"*In the quiet chambers of the soul, I am the sentinel, carving pathways where secrets hide. As the guardian of stories yet to be composed, I offer weary souls a sanctuary where their hearts find home.*"

26. Rain in the Midst of Summer

In the heart of summer's blaze,
When the earth is parched and the air scorches,
Comes a gentle murmur,
A whisper from the heavens,
As clouds gather and skies darken,
And rain begins to fall.

It's raining in the middle of summer,
A paradoxical dance of nature's whim,
Where droplets cascade like liquid diamonds,
And the scent of petrichor fills the air,
A symphony of relief amidst the sweltering heat.

Leaves glisten with newfound life,
As if each raindrop carries a secret promise,
To quench the thirst of the earth,
To revive the wilting flowers,
And to soothe the weary souls.

In this unexpected downpour,
Time slows down, and the world pauses,
As if nature herself exhales a sigh of relief,

And we, mere witnesses to her grace,
Stand in awe of the beauty,
Of rain in the midst of summer.

"In summer's blaze, rain soothes, reviving earth with liquid diamonds."

27. You Are Looking for Me and I Am Looking for Peace

In the cacophony of existence,
Amidst the hustle and the haste,
You search for me,
And I seek solace in the quiet embrace of peace.

Your eyes, restless wanderers,
Scan the crowded streets,
The bustling markets,
The echoing chambers of life,
Seeking a reflection of your soul,
In the faces of strangers,
In the depths of human connection.

But I am elusive,
A whisper in the wind,
A shadow in the night,
Drifting beyond the reach of your grasp,
Yet closer than you imagine.

And I, I am not far,

Just a breath away,
A heartbeat apart,
But obscured by the noise,
The clamor of desires,
The tumult of fears.

You are looking for me,
And I am looking for peace,
In the stillness of dawn,
In the silence of dusk,
In the gentle rhythm of the universe,
Where souls entwine,
And hearts find their home.

So let us journey together,
You and I,
Through the tangled paths of existence,
Towards the tranquil shores of serenity,
Where our quest ends,
And our spirits find rest,
In the timeless embrace of peace.

"In the rush of life, I wait in the stillness where souls meet."

28. Watching Butterfly

In the garden of fleeting moments,
Where time dances on delicate wings,
I find myself a silent observer,
Watching butterfly.

A kaleidoscope of colors,
Fluttering against the canvas of sky,
Each delicate wingbeat a testament,
To the beauty of transformation.

I am but a passerby,
In the symphony of nature's embrace,
As butterfly dances,
Amongst the blooms of life.

With every gentle sway,
Of petals kissed by sunlight,
Butterfly pirouettes,
In a ballet of grace.

In its delicate flight,
I glimpse a reflection of my own journey,
A reminder of the fragility of existence,

And the resilience of the spirit.

For in the wings of butterfly,
I see the whispers of hope,
The promise of renewal,
And the eternal dance of life.

"In the butterfly's delicate flight, I see both the fragility and resilience of my own journey, a reminder of life's eternal dance."

29. Why is it that friends elude me

In the quiet moments,
when the world is a blurred hum,
I sit with the echo of my solitude.

I am the solitary figure
wandering through the halls
of my own making,
where the shadows are my only companions
and the silence, an unforgiving mirror.

Why is it that friends elude me,
like whispers that vanish in the wind,
or dreams that dissolve in morning light?

I reach out,
only to grasp at emptiness,
fingers brushing against the chill
of invisible barriers.

It is not that I shun their presence,
but rather, that I seem
to dance on the edge

of connection,
always in motion but never arriving.

Is it that my own heart
is a labyrinth too complex
for another soul to navigate,
or am I simply a ghost
in the bustling corridors of life?

I ponder my reflection,
seeing in it not just a person,
but a question,
an enigma wrapped in the guise of flesh and blood.

In the stillness, I wonder:
Am I the keeper of a gate
that remains locked,
or merely a wanderer
in a world that spins too fast,
too indifferent?

Yet, in this introspection,
I find no clear answers,
only the soft ache of knowing
that in my solitude,
there is a kind of clarity,
a bittersweet acceptance

of the space I occupy,
alone but profoundly aware.

"In the quiet of my solitude, I ponder whether I am the keeper of a locked gate or simply a wanderer in a world too fast, too indifferent."

30. I'll talk to anyone

Amidst crowds I roam,
Words a bridge to hearts unknown,
I'll talk, I'll be known.

With open eyes, I see,
Strangers become stories,
Unwritten chapters waiting to be read,
In every face, a tale unsaid.

I'll listen to the whispers,
In the rustle of leaves,
In the hum of the city streets,
In the quiet of a forgotten bench.

To anyone, I'll extend a hand,
A smile, a nod, an understanding glance,
For in the tapestry of life,
Every thread matters, every voice stands.

From the boisterous to the shy,
In laughter or in sighs,
In every tone and every cry,
I'll be there, the bridge, the tie.

For in this world so vast,
Connections made can last,
A moment's talk, a lifetime's memory,
In anyone, I'll find a friend to see.

So amidst crowds I roam,
With words as my guide,
I'll talk, I'll be known,
In every heart, a place to reside.

31. Opinions

My opinions flutter like moths
around a flickering candle,
drawn to the light but aware of the burn.
In the corners of my mind,
they whisper, they scream,
they fight to be heard,
each one a fragment of the truth
I am still piecing together.

Sometimes, they are the echo of a childhood laugh,
pure and unfiltered,
running barefoot through the grass,
believing in the magic of ordinary things.
Other times, they are the weight of sorrow,
pressed into the lines of my face,
etched by the hands of time,
each crease a testament to lessons learned too late.

I carry them like stones in my pockets,
heavy, grounding, yet
sometimes drowning,
each one a reflection of the choices I've made,
the roads I've traveled,

the battles I've fought within my own heart.

They shape my world, color my vision,
turning the mundane into a canvas of complexity,
where every stroke is a thought,
every shade a feeling,
a never-ending blend of love and fear,
hope and regret.

And in the silence of the night,
when the world is hushed and still,
I sift through them,
these opinions of mine,
finding solace in their chaos,
a strange comfort in their familiarity,
knowing they are my compass,
my burden, my light in the dark.

32. I am dead and hollow inside

In the silence of the night, I find myself wandering,
a ghost in the shadows, an echo of what once was.
I am dead and hollow inside,
a void where life used to pulse, where dreams used to bloom.

Once, there was light in these eyes,
a spark that could ignite worlds, set hearts ablaze.
Now, they are windows to an abyss,
cold and unyielding, reflecting nothing but the emptiness within.

I remember the days when laughter was easy,
when the sun painted the world in vibrant hues,
and hope was a constant companion,
whispering sweet promises of tomorrow.

But those days have withered like autumn leaves,
crumbling to dust beneath the weight of time.
The laughter has turned to echoes,
faint and distant, lost in the corridors of my mind.

I am a vessel, emptied of joy,
a shell that walks and talks, but feels nothing.

The world around me moves in technicolor,
yet I remain in grayscale, untouched by its beauty.

Memories swirl like ghosts, haunting my every step,
reminders of a life that seems more dream than reality.
I am dead and hollow inside,
a canvas once filled with love, now marred by shadows.

There is a stillness in my heart,
a quiet that speaks of absence, of something irrevocably lost.
It is a void that swallows all light,
a black hole of sorrow that knows no end.

People pass by, their lives intertwined with purpose,
their eyes bright with the fire of existence.
I envy their passion, their connection to the world,
for I am but a spectator, watching from the fringes.

The warmth of human touch, the comfort of a kind word,
they slip through my fingers like sand,
elusive and unreachable, as if I am a specter,
destined to drift alone through the corridors of time.

I am dead and hollow inside,
a requiem of silence, a dirge of despair.
Yet, somewhere deep within, a flicker of defiance remains,
a stubborn ember that refuses to be extinguished.

Perhaps, in this vast emptiness, there is a seed of rebirth,
a chance to rise from the ashes, to reclaim the light.
But for now, I wander these shadowed halls,
a soul in limbo, searching for a way back to life.

"Amidst the shadows and echoes of a life once vibrant,
I wander, a hollow soul seeking the light of rebirth."

Emerging Voices

Introducing ***"Emerging Voices,"*** a distinguished section within our book, *Soulful Murmurs*, meticulously curated to highlight the creative endeavors of burgeoning writers. This section serves as a platform for aspiring authors to showcase their work and expand their audience. Our primary aim is to nurture and bolster emerging talents within the writing community, offering them an invaluable opportunity for exposure and recognition.

33. Echoes of Twenties

Hanging in limbo, a daily quest,
Figuring out what's life's grand jest.
Self-love, healing, in the mind they swirl,
A dance of terms, in this grown-up world.

Ambition, goals, and future stare,
Partial responsibilities, a weight to bear.
A sudden urge to rise, to take the lead,
Finish assignments, pursue the grand deed.

Birthdays tick, a reminder clear,
Parents aging, whispers in the ear.
A pact with time, a silent vow,
"Make them proud," the heartbeat now.

Actions align with a filial grace,
Reducing their toil, a loving embrace.
Earn enough to bestow all they're due,
A symphony of love, ever true.

In the labyrinth of change, one thing stands,
A sibling, a constant, holding hands.
Baby no more, a shock in the gaze,

Taunting jests, a nostalgic phase.

"You are in 10th!, do your task!"
Yet, in the heart, a wish to bask,
In moments past, the baby sis smile,
An echo in time, a cherished mile.

As life unfolds, and paths are trod,
The heart yearns for the baby sis, the demigod.
In the dance of time, a sibling's glee,
An anchor to the past, a reverie.

So here's to the journey, the twenties wild,
A symphony of growth, as the years compiled.
In every step, in each new dawn,
The heartbeat of love, forever drawn.

- Vishakha Deshpande
Instagram : @vishhaakhaa

"Discovering Vishakha's hidden writer side beyond her TechGeek persona has been a delightful revelation this year. Eagerly anticipating more from her pen, I wish her boundless success in her literary endeavors. Here's to unveiling Vishakha's verses in the book of life."

34. Fading Promises

I agree it was easier for me
to look at my corpse than it was for you;
As you watch me dissipate,
Like one of your beloved stars.

I want to remind you
That the promises I made,
I'd keep them forever;
But as time passed by,
I saw you with someone else,

I faded along with the
Promises you made to her.

- Sahiti Ramadugu
Instagram : @sahiti1331

35. Stardust

In the cosmic dance, under starlit skies,
Hearts seek the love that never dies.
To say, "I am yours," and bring a smile,
In love's embrace, life finds its sweetest ties.

Love is the thing that will never let go in the midst of the
hardships.
A bond that transcends, a spiritual light.
To be loved despite our flaws and divide,
this embrace is where our spirits really reside.

When burdens heavy and hope slight,
and despair clamps onto life,
Love tiptoes softly and gently cries,
It's I who'll turn night into light.

As days will turn into nights,
We'll grow stronger with time.
As the love between two souls ignites,
The darkness will be dispelled, divine.

With you, the cosmos unfolds in my vision, In your eyes, the
universe I see,

A reflection of eternity, just you and me,
A portrait of purest grace, In your colors, my heart finds its place.

With every heartbeat, our symphony plays,
A melody of love that forever stays.
In the dance of the cosmos, we are but a part,
Yet in each other, we've found our beating heart.

- Sujal V. Musale
Instagram : @sujalmusale8

"I have known Sujal since our +1 and +2 days of JEE preparation, and it feels wonderful to see him thriving both creatively and professionally."

36. In the Shadows of Struggle

In the shadows, I stand, battling storms within,
Anxiety's grip tight, panic's whispers begin.
Alone in a house, where freedom is a dream,
Negativity's weight, in every silent scream.

In my brother's walls, a place not quite mine,
Unwanted echoes, in the halls entwine.
A step sister's tale, in a childhood of pain,
Living with ghosts, memories like rain.

Friendless paths, left by those untrue,
Betrayal's sting, a heart split in two.
Trust shattered, in the darkness I roam,
A soul longing for light, to find its way home.

For in the depths of despair, a phoenix is vowed.

In the face of opposition, courage must rise,
For your dreams and desires, reach for the skies.
Though family may falter
Within you lies a fire, a flame in your heart.

Embrace your uniqueness, your journey, your song,
In the symphony of life, you truly belong.
Stand tall, brave soul, let your light shine bright,
In the darkest of tunnels, you'll find your own light.

Suicidal whispers, a battle within,
But know you're not alone, in this fight you'll win.

Failed attempts may darken your way,
But hope's gentle glow will light your day.
Reach out for help, let your voice be heard,
In the symphony of life, your song will be stirred.

Strength lies within, in moments of despair,
Courage to seek help, to show you care.
Your life is precious, a story to unfold,
In the tapestry of time, your worth is gold.

- Arya Katre
Instagram : @create_witharya

37. Flaw

Can a mistake define me?
How do they know that's all I've done or will do in the future?
It's like a stain on a garment that fades but never leaves.
But can a mistake define me?

How do you know where the stain came from?
What if it came from something I love?
I don't need someone reminding me of how bad it looks.

But now I understand that a mistake may define me for them.
Cause stain outside called insecurity.
And a scar inside called trauma.
They may unseen it to validate their thoughts.
But it's only a mistake which is never gonna be forget.

-Shravani Bante
Instagram : @_shravani22

38. Nostalgia

The time that Flies,
The memories that lies;
It's the nostalgia of the air,
Which we can feel in winter.

It's the story of all,
Something that we lost,
The nostalgia of the place,
Hits the heart;
The nature that we crave &
The places that we save,
It's the nostalgia again
Which we can't forget.
Have you ever got a nostalgia by a person?
That could be father, mother or lover;
It's the sign that you are living,
Grabbing this feelings.

It's the nostalgia that feels in winters
By some air, place & persons.

-Shara Tadas
Instagram : @_sharrus_26

39. Memories' Lesson

Lost in the memory's embrace,
Where smiles came easy,
And laughter knew no bounds,
Yes, I see us lost in the memories,

Where dancing in public was not a shame,
And enjoying our own company was not a burden.
Life teaches through its memories,
And the lesson I've learned is this:

It's not about competing with others,
But about cherishing those
With whom we create memories.

- Vedant Jagtap
Instagram : @vedant_.jagtap

"Vedant's verses bridge gaps where words falter. As a senior, I've seen his talent shine, conveying profound ideas with poetic finesse. Wishing Vedant a future full of poetic triumphs and boundless creativity!"

About Author

Parth Ajit Khajgiwale, celebrated for his previous work *Shades Of Reflection: Exploring Duality*, is a distinguished writer whose influence extends beyond traditional literary circles. His compelling storytelling, enriched with psychological insight and empathetic understanding, has garnered him a dedicated following on Instagram. There, he has cultivated a vibrant community of creative thinkers and engaged in meaningful dialogue with his audience.

In his latest work, *Soulful Murmurs: Verses from Unspoiled Heart*, Khajgiwale adopts a new pen name: *Parth Priti Khajgiwale*. He reflects on this choice, stating, *"The previous pen name was Parth Ajit Khajgiwale; the new one is Parth Priti Khajgiwale. I chose this name to honor both sides of my heritage. As I embrace the legacies of Priti and Ajit, my ambition is to make them both proud."* This thoughtful decision symbolizes his commitment to integrating and celebrating the diverse aspects of his identity and aspirations.

Beyond his literary achievements, Khajgiwale is a noted tech enthusiast and researcher. His tech blogs and research papers explore the transformative potential of artificial intelligence (AI) and its role in modern life. Khajgiwale advocates for a nuanced approach to technology, recognizing its value while emphasizing the need to balance emotional and practical considerations. He believes that while AI is crucial for innovation and efficiency, it should complement rather than replace the human elements of empathy and practicality.

Khajgiwale's writing is marked by his exploration of the intersection between practicality and emotion. He challenges conventional views that often pit these two aspects against each other, encouraging readers to reflect on their own experiences. His work invites readers to confront and reconcile the complexities of their emotional and practical lives, offering a space for introspection and growth.

Soulful Murmurs is designed to be a profound emotional experience rather than just an entertaining read. The book takes readers on a journey through a range of emotions, from nostalgia to introspection, aiming to provoke thought and reflection. Khajgiwale's intention is to engage readers deeply, encouraging them to navigate their own emotional landscapes with both heart and intellect.

In this book, Khajgiwale also pays tribute to the late *Shri Pralhad P. Chhabria, Founder President of the Hopes Foundation and Research Center*. Khajgiwale acknowledges Chhabria's significant influence on his life and work, noting, *"Chhabria's legacy, characterized by his commitment to impact and greatness, has been a source of inspiration and motivation for me to strive for excellence and push boundaries."* This homage underscores Khajgiwale's respect for Chhabria's enduring impact and his own aspirations to continue striving for greatness.

Soulful Murmurs: Verses from Unspoiled Heart thus represents a convergence of personal reflection and universal themes. It offers readers an opportunity to explore their own emotional and practical dimensions, encouraging a deep, introspective engagement with the text.

For more updates and interactions, you can connect with *Parth Priti Khajgiwale* on *Instagram* at *@versevirtuoso_*, or reach out via email at *parth.khajgiwale@gmailcom*.